811.5

THE ALLIGATOR BRIDE

Hall, Donald

811.5

The Alligator Bride

BOOKS BY DONALD HALL

POETRY

The Alligator Bride
A Roof of Tiger Lilies
The Dark Houses
Exiles and Marriages

PROSE

Henry Moore
String Too Short to Be Saved

Donald Hall

The Alligator Bride

Poems New and Selected

HARPER & ROW, PUBLISHERS
New York, Evanston, and London

1817

Acknowledgment is made to the following publications in which many of the poems included in this volume first appeared in somewhat different form: *Anon, Audit, Chelsea, Encounter, Fresco, The Fifties, The Harvard Advocate, Hudson Review, The Kenyon Review, The Listener, Mademoïselle Malahat Review, Michigan Quarterly Review, The Nation, National Review, New Orleans Poetry, The New Orleans Review, The New Statesman, New World Writing, The New Yorker, Partisan Review, Poetry, Saturday Review, Sumac, This World,* and *The Western Review.*

FIRST EDITION

LIBRARY OF CONGRESS CATALOG CARD NUMBER: 78-83597

for Andrew and Philippa

Contents

I Exiles

II Tiger Lilies

III   The Alligator Bride

The poems in the first section were written between 1948 and 1958, and most of them appeared in *Exiles and Marriages* (1955) and *The Dark Houses* (1958). I have revised most of these poems, and changed titles. The second part is reprinted from *A Roof of Tiger Lilies* (1964) with minor changes. The poems in the third section are previously uncollected.

D. H.

I   Exiles

Wedding Party

The pock-marked player of the accordion
Empties and fills his squeeze box in the corner,
Kin to the tiny man who pours champagne,
Kin to the caterer. These solemn men,
Amid the sounds of silk and popping corks,
Stand like pillars. And the white bride
Moves through the crowd as a chaired relic moves.

Now all at once the pock-marked player grows
Immense and terrible beside the bride
Whose marriage withers to a rind of years
And curling photographs in a dry box;
And in the storm that hurls upon the room
Above the crowd he holds his breathing box
That only empties, fills, empties, fills.

Love Is Like Sounds

Late snow fell this early morning of spring.
At dawn I rose from bed, restless, and looked
Out of my window, to wonder if there the snow
Fell outside your bedroom, and you watching.

I played my game of solitaire. The cards
Came out the same the third time through the deck.
The game was stuck. I threw the cards together,
And watched the snow that could not do but fall.

Love is like sounds, whose last reverberations
Hang on the leaves of strange trees, on mountains
As distant as the curving of the earth,
Where the snow hangs still in the middle of the air.

Old Home Day

Wilmot, New Hampshire

Under the eyeless, staring lid,
And in the pucker of a mouth,
Gullied hayfields cave together
And crumble in the August drouth.

Here man to man remembers when
Bat struck ball upon this plain,
Sixty years ago before
The batter's box washed out in rain.

Exile

A boy who played and talked and read with me
Fell from a maple tree.

I loved her, but I told her I did not,
And wept, and then forgot.

I walked the streets where I was born and grew,
And all the streets were new.

Elegy for Wesley Wells

Against the clapboards and the window panes
The loud March whines with rain and heavy wind,
In dark New Hampshire where his widow wakes.
She cannot sleep. The familiar length is gone.
I think across the clamorous Atlantic
To where the farm lies hard against the foot
Of Ragged Mountain, underneath Kearsarge.
I speak his name against the beating sea.
      His dogs will whimper through the webby barn,
Where spiders close his tools in a pale gauze
And wait for flies. The nervous woodchuck now
Will waddle plumply through the world of weeds
Eating wild peas as if he owned the land,
And the fat hedgehog rob the apple trees.
When next October's frosts harden the ground
And fasten in the year's catastrophe,
The farm will lie like driftwood,
The farmer dead, and deep in his carved earth.

Before the Civil War the land was used,
And railroads came to all the villages;
Before the war, a man with land was rich;
He cleared a thousand or two thousand acres,
Burning the timber, stacking up the stones,
And cultivated all his acreage
And planted it to vegetables to sell.
But then the war took off the hired men;
The fields grew up, to weeds and bushes first,
And then the fields were thick with ashy pine.
The faces of prosperity and luck
Turned westward with the railroads from New England.
      Poverty settled, and the first went off,

Leaving their fathers' forty-acre farms,
To Manchester and Nashua and Lowell,
And traded the Lyceum for the block.
Now the white houses fell, among the wars;
From eighteen-sixty-five, for eighty years,
The Georgian firmness sagged, and the paint chipped,
And the white houses rotted to the ground.
Great growths of timber felled grew up again
On what had once been cultivated land,
On lawns and meadows, and from cellar holes.
Deep in the forest now, half covered-up,
The reddened track of an abandoned railroad
Heaved in the frosts, in roots of the tall pines;
A locomotive stood
Like a strange rock, red as the fallen needles.

The farmer worked from four and milking time
To nine o'clock and shutting up the hens.
The heavy winter fattened him; the spring
Unlocked his arms and made his muscles lame.
By nineteen-forty, only the timid young
Remained to plough or sell; the others, strong,
Could earn a city wage.
He was the noble man in the sick place.
I number out the virtues that are dead,
Remembering his soft, consistent voice,
His gentleness, and most,
The bone that showed in each deliberate word.

     I stand alone on England's crowded shore
Where storm has driven everyone inside.
My place and people are for sure across
The hooded wind and barbarous Atlantic
In dark New Hampshire where his widow wakes.
I think across to him, old man I loved,
The tall and straight, bent in a clumsy box.

The length of Wesley Wells, those miles away,
Today was carried to the lettered plain
In Andover,
While March bent down the cemetery trees.

No Deposit   No Return

No Deposit   No Return
   Said the bottle dead of beer.
Toughly by small things we learn
   Courage in this hemisphere,
Bleak and honest to affirm
A single independent term.

It only hurts me when I laugh,
   Said the hunter crucified.
I'm not Jesus Christ by half
   So keep all weapons from my side
Or you'll take a dead man's curse;
Life is hell but death is worse.

In the caves of the Dordogne
   Paleolithic doctors made
Records with their flint and stone
   Of the slogans of the trade:
Strike the big bulls in the heart;
Leave the pregnant cows apart.

Shoot these old gray hairs, she said,
   But spare your country's flag! He thought.
Then Stonewall Jackson went ahead
   And ordered Barbara Frietchie shot.
His loyal soldiers cheered to see
This total lack of chivalry.

The hairy fetch of felt disease
   Which glories in its brutal name
Eats anguish like a Stilton cheese
   And spreads, in process, crafty blame
Until no person fouled by it
Can keep the savors separate.

Dillinger the killer died
　In a theater lobby when
One who slept at his own side
　Squealed his name to the G-Men.
His final utterance was heard
To be a single dirty word.

Chinese Gordon sat alone
　When the Mahdi broke the door;
His sword flashed twice; he stood like stone
　Until they speared him to the floor.
Two he killed before he died
Flanked him dead on either side.

Though the name of failure bray
　Like a donkey in despair,
Who must weep that jacks betray
　In the dark the darling mare,
We shall take our failures up
And drink them down from the full cup.

It only hurts me when I bray,
　Chinese Gordon said, and died.
Disease is hairier today,
　Said Barbara Frietchie crucified.
But she added from the hearse,
Life is hell but death is worse.

Dillinger spoke, and doctors drew
　Records of what the killer said,
Where Stonewall Jackson came to view
　Six pregnant cows untimely dead,
Upon whose sides one could discern
No Deposit　　　No Return.

My Son, My Executioner

My son, my executioner,
   I take you in my arms,
Quiet and small and just astir,
   And whom my body warms.

Sweet death, small son, our instrument
   Of immortality,
Your cries and hungers document
   Our bodily decay.

We twenty-five and twenty-two,
   Who seemed to live forever,
Observe enduring life in you
   And start to die together.

The Sleeping Giant

a hill in Hamden, Connecticut

The whole day long, under the walking sun
That poised an eye on me from its high floor,
Holding my toy beside the clapboard house
I looked for him, the summer I was four.

I was afraid the waking arm would break
From the loose earth and rub against his eyes
A fist of trees, and the whole country tremble
In the exultant labor of his rise;

Then he with giant steps in the small streets
Would stagger, cutting off the sky, to seize
The roofs from house and home because we had
Covered his shape with dirt and planted trees;

And then kneel down and rip with fingernails
A trench to pour the enemy Atlantic
Into our basin, and the water rush,
With the streets full and all the voices frantic.

That was the summer I expected him.
Later the high and watchful sun instead
Walked low behind the house, and school began,
And winter pulled a sheet over his head.

Christmas Eve in Whitneyville

to my father

December, and the closing of the year;
The momentary carolers complete
Their Christmas Eves, and quickly disappear
Into their houses on each lighted street.

Each car is put away in each garage;
Each husband home from work, to celebrate,
Has closed his house around him like a cage,
And wedged the tree until the tree stood straight.

Tonight you lie in Whitneyville again,
Near where you lived, and near the woods or farms
Which Eli Whitney settled with the men
Who worked at mass-producing firearms.

The main street, which was nothing after all
Except a school, a stable, and two stores,
Was improvised and individual,
Picking its way alone, among the wars.

Now Whitneyville is like the other places,
Ranch houses stretching flat beyond the square,
Same stores and movie, same composite faces
Speaking the language of the public air.

Old houses of brown shingle still surround
This graveyard where you wept when you were ten
And helped to set a coffin in the ground.
You left a friend from school behind you then,

And now return, a man of fifty-two.
Talk to the boy. Tell him about the years
When Whitneyville quadrupled, and how you
And all his friends went on to make careers,

Had cars as long as hayricks, boarded planes
For Rome and Paris where the pace was slow,
And took the time to think how yearly gains,
Profit and volume made the business grow.

"The things you had to miss," you said last week,
"Or thought you had to, take your breath away."
You propped yourself on pillows, where your cheek
Was hollow, stubbled lightly with new gray.

This love is jail; another sets us free.
Tonight the houses and their noise distort
The thin rewards of solidarity.
The houses lean together for support.

The noises fail, and lights go on upstairs.
The men and women are undressing now
To go to sleep. They put their clothes on chairs
To take them up again. I think of how,

All over Whitneyville, when midnight comes,
They lie together and are quieted,
To sleep as children sleep, who suck their thumbs,
Cramped in the narrow rumple of each bed.

They will not have unpleasant thoughts tonight.
They make their houses jails, and they will take
No risk of freedom for the appetite,
Or knowledge of it, when they are awake.

The lights go out and it is Christmas Day.
The stones are white, the grass is black and deep.
I will go back and leave you here to stay
Where the dark houses harden into sleep.

Jack and the Other Jack

Jack told himself the world was pure as soap,
The kind that floats. He traveled little, went
From home to work to home, so that his scope
Would not include corruption or dissent.

He drank no coffee, but he couldn't sleep.
Although he knelt beside his bed and prayed,
He prayed to names. His rabbit pulse would leap
To see a drunken man. He was afraid.

Then in his room it stood, face much like his,
But changed throughout, the lips and nose more wide,
A large, permanent smile whose messages
Attacked his ear with grossness. Terrified,

He waited for a metamorphosis.
The loosened body, filled with appetite,
He thought would slough all memory but this
Adjunct of novelty and bad delight.

He found himself mistaken, for in time
The long way home became his self-command;
He learned that wanting things was not a crime,
Nor was it devilish to understand.

Now unified within their father's son,
Two Jacks combine their mutual desire,
And talk each night about what they have done
And not done, and continue to conspire.

Je Suis une Table

It has happened suddenly,
by surprise, in an arbor,
or while drinking good coffee,
after speaking, or before,

that I dumbly inhabit
a density; in language,
there is nothing to stop it,
for nothing retains an edge.

Simple ignorance presents,
later, words for a function,
but it is common pretense
of speech, by a convention,

and there is nothing at all
but inner silence, nothing
to relieve on principle
now this intense thickening.

These Faces

Ignoring Rome and the Great Wall of
China, and nineteen-thirty-seven;
ignoring that years run down, men change,
buildings and machines wear out, nations
lose wars or break down after winning,
that civilizations stagger like
seasons from phase to phase; these faces
when they are old are neither tragic
nor hateful nor resigned, but puzzled
and resentful, for these men grow old
and do not know that they are older.
I cannot see the watch on my wrist
without knowing that I am dying,
and that a new politician is
being born, perhaps in Jakarta.

The Foundations of American Industry

In the Ford plant
at Ypsilanti
men named for their
fathers work at steel
machines named Bliss,
Olaffson, Smith-Grieg,
and Safety.

In the Ford plant
the generators
move quickly on
belts, a thousand now
an hour. New men
move to the belt when
the shift comes.

For the most part
the men are young, and
go home to their
Fords, and drive around,
or watch TV,
sleep, and then go work,
towards payday;

when they walk home
they walk on sidewalks
marked W
P A 38;
their old men made
them, and they walk on
their fathers.

"I Come to the Garden Alone"

Among the dead of this village church
the old women's voices use the pitch
of the pumping organ to lean on;
light comes through the trees and the dark green
curtains speckled with holes, and light hits
the frayed red cloth of the cushioned seats.

I stand among the relics of childhood
and the century before. My dead
crowd into the pew; I hear their thin
voices complain in a reedy hymn
of parch in the garden, of hunger
for rest, and of the words that I hear:

"We who do not exist make noises
only in you. Your illusion says
that we who are cheated and broken
croon our words to the living again.
You must not believe in anything;
you who feel cheated are crooning."

Christ Church Meadows, Oxford

Often I saw, as on my balcony
    I stirred the afternoon into my tea,
Enamelled swards descending to the *Thames,*
    Called *Isis* here, and flowers that were gems,
Cattle in herds, and great senescent trees,
    Through which, as Pope predicted, ran the breeze.
Ad sinistram, where limpid *Cherwell* flows,
    Often I saw the punts of gallant beaux
Who sang like shepherds to each gentle love
    Quaint tales of Trojan warriors to prove
That loving Maidens are rewarded here
    With bastards and with pints of watered beer.
Here too I saw my countrymen at large,
    Expending *Kodachrome* upon a barge.
From chauffered *Car,* or touring *Omnibus,*
    They leered at me, calling me "them," not "us."
A jutting woman came to me and said,
    "Your *Highness,* can those big white geese be fed?"
"Yankee go home," I snarled. "Of course the *Swans,*
    As the *Bard* puts it, are reserved for *Dons."*
She fainted then, beside two *Christ Church* porters,
    Who cast her, as I told them, on the waters.

By the Exeter River

"What is it you're mumbling, old Father, my Dad?
Come drink up your soup and I'll put you to bed."

"By the Exeter River, by the river, I said."

"Stop dreaming of rivers, old Father, my Dad,
Or save all your dreaming till you're tucked in bed."

"It was cold by the river. We came in a sled."

"It's colder to think of, old Father, my Dad,
Than the blankets and bolsters and pillows of bed."

"We took off his dress and the cap from his head."

"Undressed in the winter, old Father, my Dad?
What could you be thinking? Let's get off to bed."

"And Sally, poor Sally I reckon is dead."

"Was she an old sweetheart, old Father, my Dad?
Now lean on my shoulder and come up to bed."

"We drowned your half-brother. I remember we did."

Sestina

Hang it all, Ezra Pound, there is only the one sestina,
Or so I thought before, always supposing
The subject of them invariably themselves.
That is not true. Perhaps they are nearly a circle,
And they tell their motifs like party conversation,
Formally repetitious, wilfully dull,

But who are we to call recurrence dull?
It is not exact recurrence that makes a sestina,
But a compromise between a conversation
And absolute repetition. It comes from supposing
That there is a meaning to the almost-circle,
And that laws of proportion speak of more than themselves.

I think of the types of men who have loved themselves,
Who studious of their faces made them dull
To find them subtle; for the nearly-a-circle,
This is the danger. The introvert sestina
May lose its voice by childishly supposing
It holds a hearer with self-conversation.

When we are bound to a tedious conversation,
We pay attention to the words themselves
Until they lose their sense, perhaps supposing
Such nonsense is at very least less dull.
Yet if the tongue is held by a sestina,
It affirms not words but the shape of the unclosed circle.

The analogy: not the precise circle,
Nor the loose patching of a conversation
Describes the repetition of a sestina;
Predictable, yet not repeating themselves
Exactly, they are like life, and hardly dull,
And not destroyed by critical supposing.

Since there is nothing precise (always supposing)
Consider the spiraling, circular, not full-circle
As the type of existence, the dull and never dull
Predictable, general movement of conversation,
Where things seem often more, slightly, than themselves,
And make us wait for the coming, like a sestina.

And so we name the sestina's subject, supposing
Our lives themselves dwindle, an incomplete circle;
About which, conversation is not dull.

Waiting on the Corners

Glass, air, ice, light,
and winter cold.
They stand on all the corners,
waiting alone, or in
groups that talk like the air
moving branches. It
is Christmas, and a red dummy
laughs in the window
of a store. Although
the trolleys come,
no one boards them,
but everyone moves
up and down, stamping his feet,
so unemployed.
They are talking, each of them,
but it is sticks and stones
that hear them,
their plans,
exultations,
and memories of the old time.
The words fly out, over
the roads and onto
the big, idle farms, on the hills,
forests, and rivers
of America, to mix into silence
of glass, air, ice, light,
and winter cold.

The Three Movements

It is not in the books
that he is looking, nor for
a new book, nor
documents of any kind, nor
does he expect it to be like the wind,
that, when you touch it, tears
without a sound of tearing, nor
like the rain
water
that becomes
grass in the sun. He
expects that when he finds it,
it will be
like a man, visible, alive
to what has happened and what
will happen, with
firmness in its face, seeing
exactly what is, without
measure of change, and not
like documents,
or rain in the grass.

But what, he says,
if it is not
for the finding, not
what you most expect, nor even
what you dread, nothing
but the books, the endless
documents, the banked
volumes that repeat
mile after mile
their names,

their information?
Perhaps there is nothing
except the rain
water
becoming the grass, the
sustenance. What
a man should do is
accumulate
information
until he has gathered, like a
farmer, as much
as his resources can contain.

Yet perhaps, he thinks,
I speak
with knowledge, but perhaps
forgetting the movement
that intrigues
all thinking. It is
the movement which works through,
which discovers itself
in alleys, in
sleep, not
expected and not
in the books of words and phrases
nor the various paints and edges
of scenery.
It is, he says,
familiar when come upon,
glimpsed
as in a mirror
unpredicted,
and it appears
to understand. It is
like himself, only visible.

"The Scream"

from Edvard Munch's painting

Observe. Ridged, raised, tactile, the horror
of the skinned head is there. It is skinned
which had a covering-up before,
and now is nude, and is determined

by what it perceives. The blood not Christ's,
blood of death without resurrection,
winds flatly in the air. Habit foists
conventional surrender to one

response in vision, but it fails here,
where the partaking viewer is freed
into the under-skin of his fear.
Existence is laid bare, and married

to a movement of caught perception
where the unknown will become the known
as one piece of the rolling mountain
becomes another beneath the stone

which shifts now towards the happy valley
which is not prepared, as it could not
be, for the achieved catastrophe
which produces no moral upshot,

no curtain, epilogue, nor applause,
no Dame to return purged to the Manse
(the Manse is wrecked)—not even the pause,
the repose of art that has distance.

"Marat's Death"

from Edvard Munch's painting

Charlotte, "the angel of assas-
sination," is unrelaxed.
She is not deep but she is tall.

Marat is dead. The people
of France will endure his death,
l'ami du peuple and no man.

Charlotte, the will begins to
revise you to leather. How
volition hurts the skin of girls!

Marat had skin which boiled like
water on a stove. His wet
and cruel skin has one wound more.

Charlotte is standing naked
and simple above the bed.
Her body is an alphabet.

"The Kiss"

from Edvard Munch's woodcut

The backs twist with the kiss
and the mouth which is the hurt
and the green depth of it
holds plainly the hour.

The aim loses its lie.
We are victims, and we shift
in the cloyed wind, the dark
harm. No, in the thick

of rubbed numbness, and we
are the winter of the air,
and the not-nothing, blurred,
bound, motion declared.

At night, wound in the clothes
of the groomed and unendured,
where the five hands of wire
rasp, hurt me and fold,

we love. Love is a kiss
which adheres like the feet
of a green lizard to walls
whole days, and is gone.

II   Tiger Lilies

Digging

One midnight, after a day when lilies
lift themselves out of the ground while you watch them,
and you come into the house at dark
your fingers grubby with digging, your eyes
vague with the pleasure of digging,

let a wind raised from the South
climb through your bedroom window, lift you in its arms
—you have become as small as a seed—
and carry you out of the house, over the black garden,
spinning and fluttering,

and drop you in cracked ground.
The dirt will be cool, rough to your clasped skin
like a man you have never known.
You will die into the ground
in a dead sleep, surrendered to water.

You will wake suffering
a widening pain in your side, a breach
gapped in your right ribs
where a green shoot struggles to lift itself upwards
through the tomb of your dead flesh

to the sun, to the air of your garden
where you will blossom
in the shape of your own self, thoughtless
with flowers, speaking
to bees, in the language of green and yellow, white and red.

O Flodden Field

in memory of *Edwin Muir*

The learned King fought
like a fool, flanked
and outtricked, who hacked
in a corner of cousins
until the ten thousand
swords lay broken,
and the women walked
in their houses alone.

On a journey among horses,
the spirit of a man who died
only a week ago
is walking through heather
and forgets that its body
had seventy years.
Wild horses are singing,
and voices of the rocks.

The spirit from the bone-yard
finds a new life, in the field
where the King's wound
built the blackness of Glasgow
and the smoke of the air.
The spirit, like a boy,
picks up from the heather
a whole sword.

"Reclining Figure"

from Henry Moore's sculpture

Then the knee of the wave
turned to stone.

By the cliff of her flank
I anchored,

in the darkness of harbors
laid-by.

"King and Queen"

from Henry Moore's sculpture

As they grew older,
the land which had grown wheat
washed down the hill,
and the river
carried the land into the sea.

The priest with the horned
mask, who brought meat
from the altar,
turned into a bird
and flew among mountains.

The people of the markets
who touched their heads to the ground,
changed into clumps of weed
among the gutters
of the bare hill.

The King and Queen rule
over the dark nation
of thrones. As slowly
as a river builds a delta,
they have become still.

"Internal and External Forms"

from Henry Moore's sculpture

What the birds say
is colored. Shade
feels the thickness
shrubs make in a
July growth,

heavy brown thorns
for Autumn, curled
horns in double
rows. Listening
the birds fly

down, in shade. Leaves
of darkness turn
inward, noises
curve inward, and
the seed talks.

The Idea of Flying

The wings lacking a trunk
flap like a sail. Body
strains, follows and stiffens the
meeting of grand jellies.

It weighs air. In the wind,
blank at the low margin,
high cuts in solids of
wind are the stone footsteps.

Unbent, loosed in the thick
sky and the walked heaven,
look, how the body of
space is a steep dying.

The Jealous Lovers

When he lies in the night away from her,
the backs of his eyelids burn.
He turns in the darkness as if it were an oven.
The flesh parches and he lies awake
thinking of everything wrong.

In the morning when he goes to meet her,
his heart struggles at his ribs
like an animal trapped in its burrow.
Then he sees her running to meet him,
red-faced with hurry and cold.

She stumbles over the snow.
Her knees above orange knee-socks
bob in a froth of the hems
of skirt and coat and petticoat.
Her eyes have not shut all night.

An Airstrip in Essex, 1960

It is a lost road into the air.
It is a desert
among sugar beets.
The tiny wings
of the Spitfires of nineteen-forty-one
flake in the mud of the Channel.

Near the road a brick pillbox
totters under a load of grass,
where Home Guards waited
in the white fogs of the invasion winter.

Goodnight, old ruined war.

In Poland the wind rides on a jagged wall.
Smoke rises from the stones; no, it is mist.

Self-portrait, As a Bear

Here is a fat animal, a bear
that is partly a dodo.
Ridiculous wings hang at his shoulders
while he plods in the brickyards
at the edge of the city, smiling
and eating flowers. He eats them
because he loves them
because they are beautiful
because they love him.
It is eating flowers which makes him fat.
He carries his huge stomach
over the gutters of damp leaves
in the parking lots in October,
but inside that paunch
he knows there are fields of lupine
and meadows of mustard and poppy.
He encloses sunshine.
Winds bend the flowers
in combers across the valley,
birds hang on the stiff wind,
at night there are showers, and the sun
lifts through a haze every morning
of the summer in the stomach.

In the Kitchen of the Old House

In the kitchen of the old house, late,
I was making some coffee
    and I daydreamed sleepily of old friends.
Then the dream turned. I waited.
    I walked alone all day in the town
where I was born. It was cold,
    a Saturday in January
when nothing happens. The streets
    changed as the sky grew dark around me.
The lamps in the small houses
    had tassels on them, and the black cars
at the curb were old and square.
    A ragman passed with his horse, their breaths
blooming like white peonies,
    and I turned into a darker street
and I recognized the house
    from snapshots. I felt as separate
as if the city and the house
    were closed inside a globe which I shook
to make it snow. No sooner
    did I think of snow, but snow started
to fill the heavy darkness
    around me. It reflected the glare
of the streetlight as it fell
    melting on the warmth of the sidewalk
and frozen on frozen grass.
    Then I heard out of the dark the sound
of steps on the bare cement
    in a familiar rhythm. Under
the streetlight, bent to the snow,
    hatless, younger than I, so young that

I was not born, my father
        walked home to his bride and his supper.
A shout gathered inside me
        like a wind, to break the rhythm,
to keep him from entering
        that door—but I stood under
a tree, closed in by the snow,
        and did not shout, to tell what happened
in twenty years, in winter,
        when his early death grew inside him
like snow piling on the grass.
        He opened the door and met the young
woman who waited for him.

The Days

Ten years ago this minute, he possibly sat
in the sunlight, in Connecticut, in an old chair:
a car may have stopped in the street outside;
he may have turned his head; his ear may have itched.
Since it was September, he probably saw
single leaves dropping from the maple tree.
If he was reading, he turned back to his book,
and perhaps the smell of roses in a pot
came together with the smell of cheese sandwiches
and the smell of a cigarette
smoked by his brother who was not dead then.

The moments of that day dwindled
to the small notations of clocks,
and the day busily became another day,
and another, and today, when his hand moves
from his ear which still itches
to rest on his leg, it is marked with the passage
of ten years. Suddenly he has the idea
that thousands and thousands of his days
lie stacked into the ground
like leaves, or like that pressure of green
which turns into coal in a million years.

Though leaves rot, or leaves burn in the gutter;
though the complications of this morning's breakfast
dissolve in faint shudders of light
at a great distance, he continues to daydream
that the past is a country under the ground
where the days practice their old habits
over and over, as faint and persistent

as cigarette smoke in an airless room.
He wishes he could travel there like a tourist
and photograph the unseizable days
in the sunlight, in Connecticut, in an old chair.

The Snow

Snow is in the oak.
Behind the thick, whitening
air which the wind drives,
the weight of the sun
presses the snow
on the pane of my window.

I remember snows and my walking
through their first fall in cities,
asleep or drunk
with the slow, desperate falling.
The snow blurs in my eyes
with other snows.

Snow is what must
come down, even if it struggles
to stay in the air with the strength
of the wind. Like an old man,
whatever I touch I turn
to the story of death.

Snow is what fills
the oak, and what covers
the grass and the bare garden.
Snow is what reverses
the sidewalk and the lawn
into the substance of whiteness.

So the watcher sleeps himself
back to the baby's eyes.
The tree, the breast, and the floor
are limbs of him, and from
his eyes he extends a skin
which grows over the world.

The baby is what must
have fallen, like snow. He resisted,
the way the old man
struggles inside the airy tent
to keep on breathing.
Birth is the fear of death.

Snow is what melts.
I cannot open the door
to the cycles of water.
The sun has withdrawn itself
and the snow keeps falling,
and something will always be falling.

The Farm

Standing on top of the hay
in a good sweat,
I felt the wind from the lake,
dry on my back,
where the chaff
grew like the down on my face.

At night on the bare boards
of the kitchen
we stood while the old man
in his nightshirt gummed
the stale crusts
of his bread and milk.

Up on the gray hill
behind the barn, the stones
had fallen away
where the Pennacook marked
a way to go
south from the narrow river.

By the side of the lake
my dead uncle's rowboat rots
in heavy bushes.
Slim pickerel glint
in the water. Black horned pout
doze on the bottom.

The Child

He lives among a dog,
a tricycle, and a friend.
Nobody owns him.

He walks by himself, beside
the black pool, in the cave
where icicles of rock

rain hard water,
and the walls are rough
with the light of stone.

He hears low talking
without words.
The hand of a wind touches him.

He walks until he is tired
or somebody calls him.
He leaves right away.

When he plays with his friend
he stops suddenly
to hear the black water.

The Kill

Sheep move on the grass
so little one imagines
small boulders.

Then a dog hurtles
into the field, like water.

The sheep flutter.
The dog tears among them
for five minutes. Then he diminishes

like a wind or a flood
into the rubble of distance.

The Wives

If I said, "Little wives,
shut in your dark
houses, an enormous
tiger lily splits
the roof of each house

in the night, and arranges
the moon to itself,
and only withdraws
just at dawn,"
you would smile,

and think about bright
flowers, and forget
the money and the shopping,
but if I went on, "I only
see your lilies grow

in my happy sleep,
because you have made no gardens
in your blocks of houses
for flowers that come
in the dark night,"

you would suddenly
cry, or pick up a book,
or walk by yourselves
for a long time
on the white sidewalks.

The Wreckage

At the edge of the city the pickerel
vomits and dies. The river
with its white hair staggers to the sea.

My life lay open like a smashed car.

Windows barred, ivy, square stone.
Lines gather at her mouth and her eyes
like cracks in a membrane.
While I watch, eyeballs and tongue
spill on the tiled floor
in a puddle of yolks and whites.

The intact 707
under the clear wave, the sun shining.

The playhouse of my grandfather's mother
stands north of the shed; spiders
and the dolls' teacups of dead women.
In Ohio the K-Mart shrugs;
it knows it is going to die.

A stone, the closed eye of the dirt.

I walked outside before dawn
past closed houses thick with breath.
A door clicked; a light opened.
Houses sailed up
like wrecks from the bottom of the sea.

But if the world is a dream
the puffed stomach of Juan is a dream
and the rich in Connecticut are dreaming.

There are poor bachelors
who live in shacks made of oilcans

and broken doors, who stitch their shirts
until the cloth disappears under stitches,
who collect nails in tin cans.

The wind is exhausted.

In the middle of the road of my life
I wake walking in a field.
A trolley car comes out of the elms,
the tracks laid through an acre of wheat stubble,
slanting downhill. I board it,
and cross the field into the new pine.

The Poem

It discovers by night
what the day hid from it.
Sometimes it turns itself
into an animal.
In summer it takes long walks
by itself where meadows
fold back from ditches.
Once it stood still
in a quiet row of machines.
Who knows
what it is thinking?

The Stump

1

Today they cut down the oak.
Strong men climbed with ropes
in the brittle tree.
The exhaust of a gasoline saw
was blue in the branches.

The oak had been dead a year.
I remember the great sails of its branches
rolling out green, a hundred and twenty feet up,
and acorns thick on the lawn.
Nine cities of squirrels lived in that tree.

Yet I was happy that it was coming down.
"Let it come down!" I kept saying to myself
with a joy that was strange to me.
Though the oak was the shade of old summers,
I loved the guttural saw.

2

By night a nude trunk stands up fifteen feet,
There are cords of firewood
on the twiggy frozen grass of the yard.
A man comes every afternoon for a week
to cut the trunk down to the grass.

Bluish stains spread through the wood
and make it harder to cut.
He says they are the nails of a trapper
who dried his pelts on the oak
when badgers dug in the lawn.

At the bottom he hacks for two days,
his knuckles scraping the stiff snow.
His chain saw breaks three teeth.
He cannot make the trunk smooth. He leaves
one night after dark.

3

Roots stiffen under the ground
and the frozen street, coiled around pipes and wires.
The stump is a platform of blond wood.
It is a door into the underground of old summers,
but if I bend down to it, I am lost
in crags and buttes of a harsh landscape
that goes on forever. When snow melts
the wood darkens into the ground;
rain and thawed snow move deeply into the stump,
backwards along the disused tunnels.

4

The edges of the trunk turn black.
In the middle there is a pale overlay,
like a wash of chalk on darkness.
The desert of the winter
has moved inside.
I do not step on it now, I am used to it,
like a rock, or a bush that does not grow.

There is a sailing ship
beached in the cove of a small island
where the warm water is turquoise.
The hulk leans over, full of rain and sand,
and shore flowers grow from it.
Then it is under full sail in the Atlantic,
on a blue day, heading for the island.

She has planted sweet alyssum
in the holes where the wood was rotten.
It grows thick, it bulges
like flowers contending from a tight vase.
Now the stump sinks downwards into its roots
with a cargo of rain
and white blossoms that last into October.

The Old Pilot

in memory of Philip Thompson

He discovers himself on an old airfield.
He thinks he was there before,
but rain has washed out the lettering of a sign.
A single biplane, all struts and wires,
stands in the long grass and wildflowers.
He pulls himself into the narrow cockpit
although his muscles are stiff
and sits like an egg in a nest of canvas.
He sees that the machine gun has rusted.
The glass over the instruments
has broken, and the red arrows are gone
from his gas gauge and his altimeter.
When he looks up, his propeller is turning,
although no one was there to snap it.
He lets out the throttle. The engine catches
and the propeller spins into the wind.
He bumps over holes in the grass,
and he remembers to pull back on the stick.
He rises from the land in a high bounce
which gets higher, and suddenly he is flying again.
He feels the old fear, and rising over the fields
the old gratitude. In the distance, circling
in a beam of late sun like birds migrating,
there are the wings of a thousand biplanes.

New Hampshire

A bear sleeps in a cellar hole; pine needles
heap over a granite doorstep; a well brims
with acorns and the broken leaves of an oak
which grew where an anvil rusted in a forge.

Inside an anvil, inside a bear, inside a leaf,
a bark of rust grows on the tree of a gas pump;
EAT signs gather like leaves in the shallow
cellars of diners; a wildcat waits for deer

on the roof of a car. Blacktop buckled by frost
starts goldenrod from the highway. Fat honey bees
meander among raspberries, where a quarrel
of vines crawls into the spilled body of a plane.

The Grass

Under grass,
among stones and the downward
probe of trees,
everything builds

or alters itself.
I am led
through a warm descent
with my eyes covered,

to hear the words
of water. I listen, with
roots of
the moist grass.

The Long River

The musk-ox smells
in his long head
my boat coming. When
I feel him there,
intent, heavy,

the oars make wings
in the white night,
and deep woods are close
on either side
where trees darken.

I rowed past towns
in their black sleep
to come here. I rowed
by northern grass
and cold mountains.

The musk-ox moves
when the boat stops,
in hard thickets. Now
the wood is dark
with old pleasures.

Sleeping

The avenue rises towards a city of white marble.
I am not meeting anyone. The capitol is empty.
I enter the dome of sleep.

. . .

My own death was drifting near me
in the middle of life. The strong body
blurred and diminished into the water.
The flesh floated away.

. . .

The shadow is a tight passage
that no one will be spared
who goes down
to the deep well.
In sleep, something remembers.
Three times since I woke
from the first sleep,
it has drunk that water.
Awake, it is still sleeping.

Wells

I lived in a dry well
under the rank grass of a meadow.

A white ladder leaned out of it
but I was afraid of the sounds

of animals grazing.
I crouched by the wall ten years

until the circle of a woman's darkness
moved over mine like a mouth.

The ladder broke out in leaves
and fruit hung from the branches.

I climbed to the meadow grass.
I drank from the well of cattle.

III   The Alligator Bride

The Blue Wing

She was all around me
like a rainy day,
and though I walked bareheaded
I was not wet. I walked
on a bare path
singing light songs
about women.

A blue wing tilts at the edge of the sea.

The wreck of the small
airplane sleeps
drifted to the high tide line,
tangled in seaweed, green
glass from the sea.

The tiny skeleton inside
remembers the falter of engines, the
cry without
answer, the long dying
into
and out of the sea.

The Alligator Bride

The clock of my days winds down.
The cat eats sparrows outside my window.
Once, she brought me a small rabbit
which we devoured together, under
the Empire Table
while the men shrieked
repossessing the gold umbrella.

Now the beard on my clock turns white.
My cat stares into dark corners
missing her gold umbrella.
She is in love
with the Alligator Bride.

Ah, the tiny fine white
teeth! The Bride, propped on her tail
in white lace
stares from the holes
of her eyes. Her stuck-open mouth
laughs at minister and people.

On bare new wood
fourteen tomatoes,
a dozen ears of corn,
six bottles of white wine,
a melon,
a cat,
broccoli
and the Alligator Bride.

The color of bubble gum,
the consistency of petroleum jelly,
wickedness oozes
from the palm of my left hand.

My cat licks it.
I watch the Alligator Bride.

Big houses like shabby boulders
hold themselves tight
in gelatin.
I am unable to daydream.
The sky is a gun aimed at me.
I pull the trigger.
The skull of my promises
leans in a black closet, gapes
with its good mouth
for a teat to suck.

A bird flies back and forth
in my house that is covered by gelatin
and the cat leaps at it
missing. Under the Empire Table
the Alligator Bride
lies in her bridal shroud.
My left hand
leaks on the Chinese carpet.

The Train

Out of memory, a long shape
of darkness, tunnel
huddled with voices, hunger
of dead trees, angels:
a green train
curves away, a head
leans from a window,
an arm
waves. The train curves tightening
the light hair to itself
and diminishes
on a Sunday morning down
the track forever,
into memory, the tunnel
of dead trees.

Make Up

The daughter with breasts
says: Daylight
covered with lazy
moss barks
like a fox farm.

The man in the brown suit
with many buttons
hides: Puns,
dreams, the body
gradually naked.

The blue air
of the forest grows
over: Ghost
stone, and the stone
daughter.

The Coal Fire

A coal fire burned in a basket grate.
We lay in front of it
while ash collected on the firebrick
like snow.
I looked at you, in the small light
of the coal fire: back
delicate, yet with the form of the skeleton,
cheekbones and chin
carved, mouth full,
and breasts like hills of flowers.

The fire was tight and small and endured
when we added a chunk every hour.
The new piece blazed at first
from the bulky shadow of fire,
turning us bright and dark.
Old coals red at the center
warmed us all night.
If we watched all night
we could not tell the new coal
when it flaked into ash.

Sew

She kneels on the floor, snip snip
in the church of scraps,
tissue like moth's wings,
pins in the cushion of her mouth,
basting and hemming
until it stands up like a person
made out of whole cloth.

Still, I lie folded
on the bolt in the dark warehouse,
dreaming my shapes.

Swan

December, nightfall at three-thirty.
I climb Mill Hill
past hawthorn and wild cherry,
mist in the hedgerows.
Smoke blows
from the orange edges of fire
working the wheat
stubble. "Putting
the goodness back,
into the soil."

2

Driving; the fog
matted around the headlights;
suddenly, a thudding
white shape in the whiteness,
running huge and frightened, lost
from its slow stream . . .

3

The mill drew up to power
the dark underneath it
through tunnels like the roots of a beech
that spread to the poles
and down to the center of the earth.

Fire breaks out in the fields.
The wheel of the mill does not turn.

Fog stacked in the hedges.

The windmill
flies, clattering its huge wings, to the swamp.
I make out cliffs of the Church,
houses drifting like glaciers.

4

I envy the man hedging and ditching,
trimming the hawthorn, burning branches
while wasps circle in the smoke of their nest,
clearing a mile of lane, patches of soot
like closed holes to a cave of fire,
the man in his cottage
who smokes his pipe in the winter, in summer
digging his garden in ten o'clock light,
the man grafted entirely to rain and air,
stained dark
by years of hedging and ditching.

5

The close-packed surface of the roots
of a root-bound plant
when I break the pot away,
the edges white
and sleek as a swan . . .

Old Houses

Old houses were scaffolding once
and workmen whistling.

The wrecker's crowbar
splits clapboard and frame;
his chisel piles bricks.
The hole he makes
rain fills. A new apartment
grows from the rain.

The wrecker whistles as loud
as the old whistling that bends
out with the nails.

Pictures of Philippa

"Here she comes
the Queen of Moons!
and Stars."

With orange hair, blue eyes and yellow breasts
she floats
smiling
on the triangular balloon
of her dress.

A Star
juts from a pedestal on
top of her head.

2

A pink blob with one red
eye, an orange
pig's nose, blue hair and beard
over a yellow mouth: "This
is Daddy when he
was born."

3

The flower sings tenor
under
his black moustache
and sounds come out
yellow; his great head
rises
from a thin stem.

The moon Queen!
stares with her lucid eyes
loving him.

"Good-bye.
Take care of not getting your hair wet."

This Room

1

When I woke this morning,
the tide of sleep
withdrawn,
my body lay white on the shore.
I rose from my body
in my fortieth year,
and came to this room.

2

point of ice hard
as diamond
in the center of stone
frozen in crystal
in the black universe moving
a million miles a second
away from the sun

3

Climbing the brown stairs
of the air, I enter
my place. I am welcomed
by pots of geraniums, green stems
thick as a thumb, uprushing
leaves! I live
in your exhalations, sweet
tongued flowers!

The Repeated Shapes

I have visited Men's Rooms
in several bars
with the rows
of urinals like old men
and the six-sided odor

of disinfectant.
I have felt the sadness
of the small white tiles,
the repeated shapes
and the unavoidable whiteness.

They are my uncles,
these old men
who are only plumbing,
who throb with tears all night
and doze in the morning.

Woolworth's

My whole life has led me here.

Daisies made out of resin,
hairnets and submarines,
sandwiches, diaries, green
garden chairs,
and a thousand boxes of cough drops.

Three hundred years ago I was hedging
and ditching in Devon.

I lacked freedom of worship,
and freedom to trade molasses
for rum, for slaves, for molasses.

"I will sail to Massachusetts
to build the Kingdom
of Heaven on Earth!"

The side of a hill
swung open.
It was Woolworth's!

I followed this vision to Boston.

Apples

They have gone
into the green hill, by doors without hinges,
or lifting city
manhole covers to tunnels
lined with grass,
their skin soft as grapes, their faces like apples.

The peacock
feather, its round eye, sees dancers underground.
The curved spot on this
apple is a fat camel, is a
fly's shadow,
is the cry of a marigold. Looking hard,

I enter:
I am caught in the web of a gray apple,
I struggle inside
an immense apple of blowing sand,
I blossom
quietly from a window-box of apples.

For one man
there are seven beautiful ladies with buns
and happy faces
in yellow dresses with green sashes
to bring him
whiskey. The rungs of a ladder tell stories

to his friend.
Their voices like apples brighten in the wind.
Now they are dancing
with fiddles and ladies and trumpets
in the round
hill of the peacock, in the resounding hill.

Crew-cuts

Men with crew-cuts
are impossible, like
ice shows. In airport bars, all winter,
holding stand-by tickets,
they wait for a plane into the next territory
and confess
to puzzlement
over the Oriental mind.

Later, they want to drop eggs on the Russians.
Later, they want
to keep violence out of the streets
by installing a machine-gun-nest on every corner.
When they talk about women, they are discussing
a subjugated race
rumored to have cached away
huge quantities of ammunition.
They lounge on the porch of the Planter's Club,
in darkest Africa,
pith helmets over their crew-cuts, drinking pink gins,
and laughing at jokes about the stupid natives,

while the tom-toms start to beat
in a million kitchens,
and the sky lightens
with a storm of Russians with hair
down to their shoulders,
as inscrutable as the Chinese,
and as merciless
as women.

Light Passage

Light
grunts out of black tubes
onto the street. It sniffs
for sausage
or cabbages that have been abandoned.

Ann Page, keep your hands to yourself.

A column of water
miles long
moves, suddenly, to the faucet.

An old gentleman finishes eating
his newspaper.
He hears the milkman's horse
backfire.
He closed his wife's eyes.

The moon is a telephone,
the hairy tree,
the perplexity of Ann Page

when darkness comes,
and the pigs of daylight.

The Grave, The Well

Taking off from Kennedy
in December, from the
airplane, I look at streetlights
below: hovering, unfixed
sockets of light.

Then darkness: Pennsylvania,
Ohio. Yellow headlights
steer slowly along macadam
outstate roads,
far from pianos and theaters.

Women are leaning back in taxis.
Men stoop into taxis
after them, and enter the
grave, the well, the mine
of fur and scent.

The Table

Walking back to the farm from the depot,
Riley slapped flies with his tail.
Twilight. Crickets scraped
in the green standing hay by the road.
The voice of my grandfather
spoke through a motion of gnats.
I held his hand. I entered
the sway of a horse.
                        At the brown table
I propped books on each other.
All morning in the room my skin
took into itself small discs
of coolness.
Then I walked in the cut hayfield
by the barn, and lay alone
in the little valley of noon heat,
in the village of little sounds.
Grasshoppers
tickled my neck and I let them.
I turned into the other world
that lives in the air. Clouds passed
like motes.
                My grandfather
clanked up the road on his mowing machine,
behind Riley dark with sweat.
I ran to the barn
and carried a bucket of water
to the loose jaws working
in the dark stall. For lunch
I sliced an onion.
Then we raked hay into mounds

and my grandfather pitched it up
where I tucked it in place on the hayrack.
My skin dried in the sun. Wind
caught me in clover.
The slow ride
back to the barn, I dangled
legs over split-pole rails
while my grandfather talked forever
in a voice that wrapped me around
with love that asked for nothing.
In my room I drank well-water
that whitened the sides of a tumbler
and coolness gathered like dark
inside my stomach.
                    This morning
I walk to the shaded bedroom and lean
on the drop-leaf table.
                    The table hums
a song to itself without sense
and I hear the voice of the heaving
ribs of Riley
and grasshoppers
haying the fields of the air.

Happy Times

There is straw in the goose bindery.
Egg princesses hear
tiny electric feet of sample witches
in the white city of bacon.
Tongues, tongues, they grow on the porch.

Mattresses lumber through the Simian Quarter,
ablaze. "Karen, the walnuts
are bothering me!" The caboose dwindles
which I fabricated of worn fruit punch.
I have eaten the fur hats.

Buick of yellow leaves, sing the peanut wheel!
While the fiddle dances
to the newspaper that regards it,
the smiles of important shrimp
shine like motors in the cabbage light.

Mount Kearsarge

Great blue mountain! Ghost.
I look at you
from the porch of the farmhouse
where I watched you all summer
as a boy. Steep sides, narrow flat
patch on top—
you are clear to me
like the memory of one day.
Blue! Blue!
The top of the mountain floats
in haze.
I will not rock on this porch
when I am old. I turn my back on you,
Kearsarge, I close
my eyes, and you rise inside me,
blue ghost.

The Man in the Dead Machine

High on a slope in New Guinea
the Grumman Hellcat
lodges among bright vines
as thick as arms. In 1942,
the clenched hand of a pilot
glided it here
where no one has ever been.

In the cockpit the helmeted
skeleton sits
upright, held
by dry sinews at neck
and shoulder, and webbing
that straps the pelvic cross
to the cracked
leather of the seat, and the breastbone
to the canvas cover
of the parachute.

Or say that the shrapnel
missed him, he flew
back to the carrier, and every
morning takes his chair, his pale
hands on the black arms, and sits
upright, held
by the firm webbing.

The Corner

It does not know
its name. It sits
in a damp corner,
spit hanging
from its chin, odor of urine
puddled around.
Huge, hairless, grunting,
it plays with itself,
sleeps, stares for hours,
and leaps
to smash itself on the wall.
Limping, bloody, falling back
into the corner, it
will not die.

The Dump

The trolley has stopped long since.
There is no motorman.
He thinks he is at the end of the line.
No, it is past the end. Around him
is the graveyard of trolleys,
thousands of oblongs, tilted
at angles to each other,
yellow paint chipped.
Stepping outside, he sees smoke rising
from holes in roofs.
Old men live here, in narrow houses full of rugs,
in this last place.

Lovers in Middle Age

The young girls look up
as we walk past the line at the movie,
and go back to examining their fingernails.

Their boyfriends are combing their hair,
and chew gum
as if they meant to insult us.

Today we made love all day.
I look at you. You are smiling at the sidewalk,
dear wrinkled face.

Waters

A rock drops in a bucket;
sudden fierce
waves exhaust themselves
against the tin circle.

A rock in a pond;
a fast
splash, and ripples move out
interrupted by weeds.

The lake enormous and calm;
a stone falls;
for an hour the surface
moves, holding to itself the frail

shudders of its skin. Stones
on the dark bottom
make the lake calm,
the life worth living.

Gold

Pale gold of the walls, gold
of the centers of daisies, yellow roses
pressing from a clear bowl. All day
we lay on the huge bed, my hand
stroking the deep
gold of your thighs and your back.
We slept and woke
entering the golden room together,
lay down in it breathing
quickly, then
slowly again,
caressing and dozing, your hand sleepily
touching my hair now.

We made in those days
tiny identical rooms inside our bodies
which the men who uncover our graves
will find in a thousand years
shining and whole.